ORTHOCONES

ANCIENT MARINE LIFE

BY KATE MOENING
ILLUSTRATIONS BY MAT EDWARDS

EPIC

BELLWETHER MEDIA • MINNEAPOLIS, MN

EPIC

EPIC BOOKS are no ordinary books. They burst with intense action, high-speed heroics, and shadows of the unknown. Are you ready for an Epic adventure?

This edition first published in 2024 by Bellwether Media, Inc.

No part of this publication may be reproduced in whole or in part without written permission of the publisher. For information regarding permission, write to Bellwether Media, Inc., Attention: Permissions Department, 6012 Blue Circle Drive, Minnetonka, MN 55343.

Library of Congress Cataloging-in-Publication Data

LC record for Orthocones available at: https://lccn.loc.gov/2023034707

Text copyright © 2024 by Bellwether Media, Inc. EPIC and associated logos are trademarks and/or registered trademarks of Bellwether Media, Inc.

Editor: Betsy Rathburn   Series Designer: Jeffrey Kollock   Book Designer: Laura Sowers

Printed in the United States of America, North Mankato, MN.

TABLE OF CONTENTS

WHAT WERE ORTHOCONES?	4
THE LIVES OF ORTHOCONES	10
FOSSILS AND EXTINCTION	16
GET TO KNOW ORTHOCONES	20
GLOSSARY	22
TO LEARN MORE	23
INDEX	24

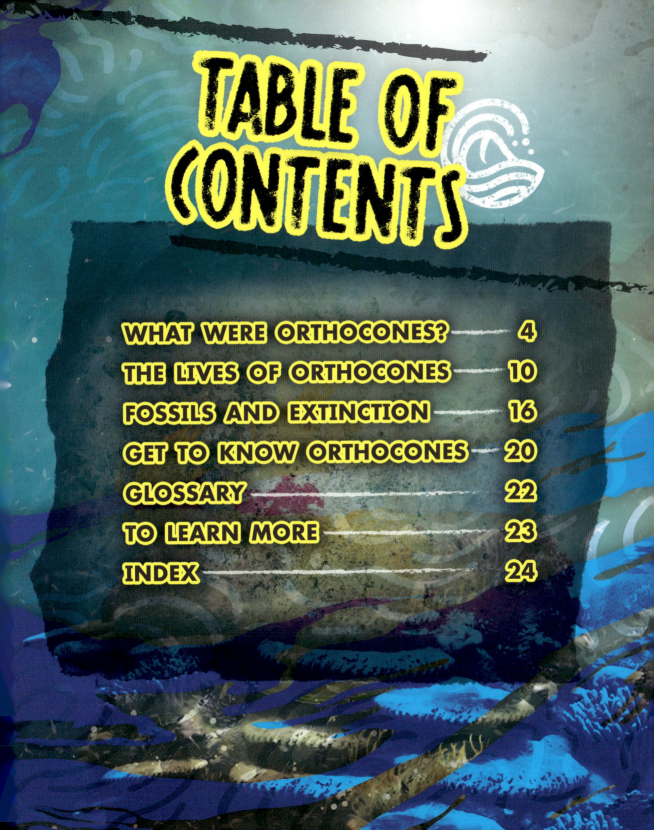

WHAT WERE ORTHOCONES?

PRONUNCIATION
OR-thoh-CONE

4

MAP OF THE WORLD

Late Cambrian period

Orthocones were **cephalopods**. They had straight, cone-shaped shells. There were many types of orthocones. They lived across many time periods. They first appeared in the Late **Cambrian period**. This was during the **Paleozoic era**.

hard shell

Orthocones came in all sizes. The biggest were over 18 feet (5.5 meters) long!

They had long **tentacles** and big eyes. Their mouths had hard **beaks**. Hard shells covered their soft bodies.

tentacles

eye

SIZE COMPARISON

about as long as a moving truck

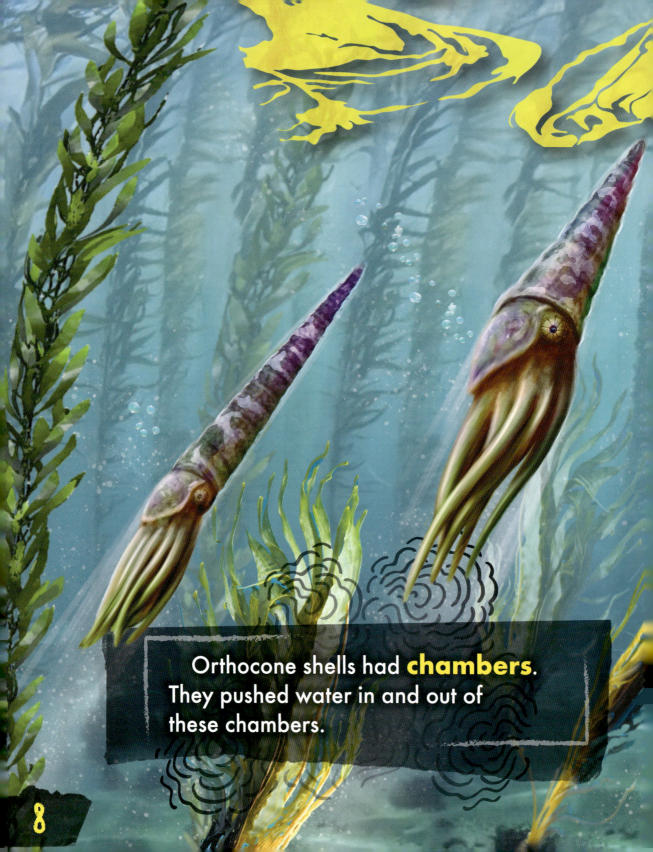

Orthocone shells had **chambers**. They pushed water in and out of these chambers.

This helped the animals move. They mostly swam up and down.

THE LIVES OF ORTHOCONES

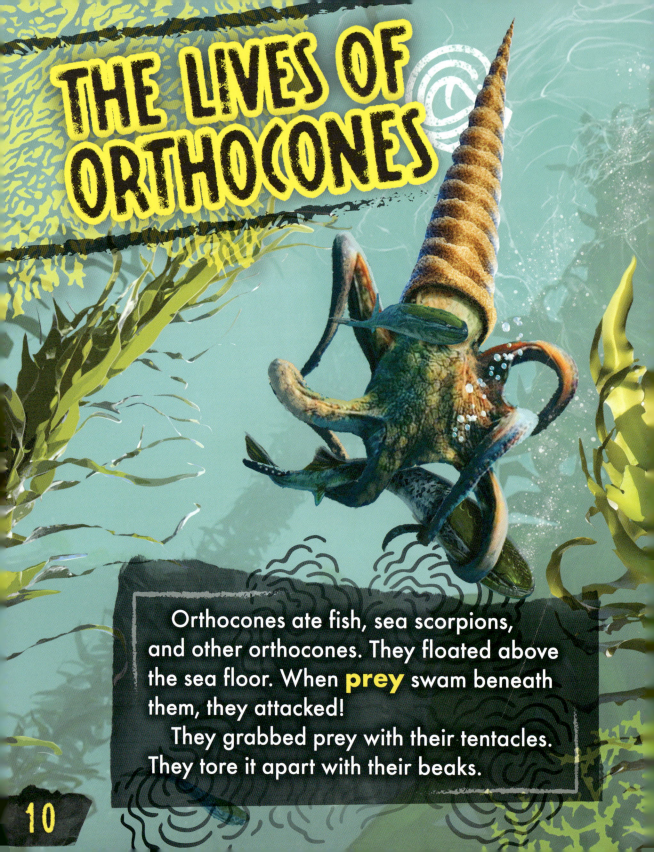

Orthocones ate fish, sea scorpions, and other orthocones. They floated above the sea floor. When **prey** swam beneath them, they attacked!

They grabbed prey with their tentacles. They tore it apart with their beaks.

TAKING IT SLOW

Orthocones were likely slow swimmers. They did not often hunt down meals. It was easier to wait for prey to swim by.

beak

ORTHOCONE DIET

fish

sea scorpions

orthocones

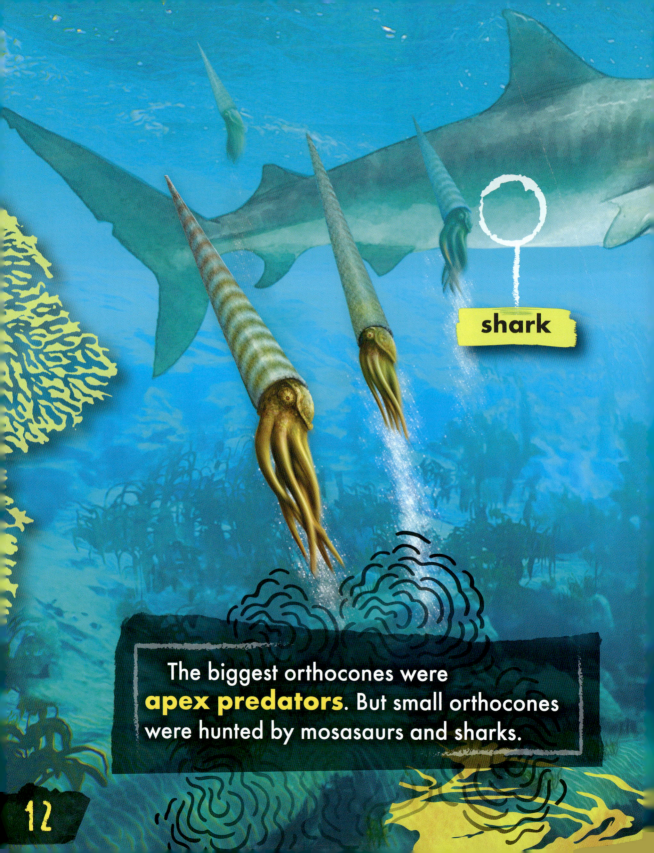

shark

The biggest orthocones were **apex predators**. But small orthocones were hunted by mosasaurs and sharks.

To stay safe, orthocones hid in their shells. They also escaped by shooting water out of their shells. They shot up to safety.

Orthocones laid many eggs at a time. Young orthocones had narrower shells than adults.

young orthocone

This likely let young move around more quickly. They could more easily chase down prey!

SHELL SHAPES

Most cephalopods today do not have shells. But a few have shells with a curled shape!

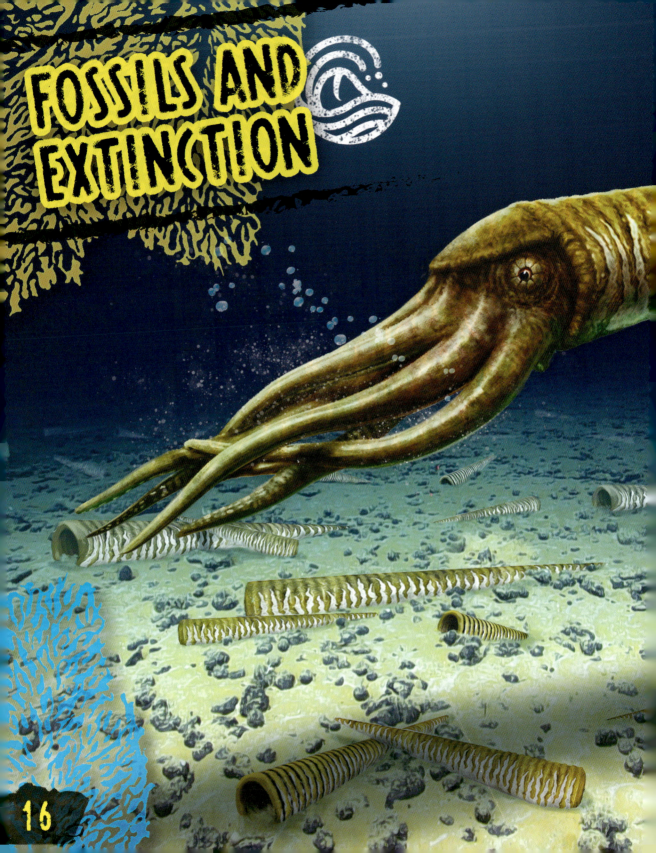

FOSSILS AND EXTINCTION

About 200 million years ago, Earth's oceans changed. Orthocones went **extinct**.
Millions of years later, new orthocones **evolved**. They lived until the oceans changed again. The last orthocones died out millions of years ago.

Orthocone **fossils** have been found all over the world. A scientist first wrote about them in 1732.

fossils

COMMON ORTHOCONE FOSSILS IN THE UNITED STATES

orthocone fossils

FOUND since the 1800s

LOCATED many states in the United States

Scientists still do not know a lot about orthocones. They are uncovering the mysteries of these special cephalopods!

GET TO KNOW ORTHOCONES

big eyes

tentacles

FOOD
- fish
- sea scorpions
- orthocones

SIZE largest over 18 feet (5.5 meters) long

ERA
first appeared about 485 million to 200 million years ago, during the Late Cambrian period

Paleozoic — **Cambrian** — **Mesozoic** — **Cenozoic**

cone-shaped shell

LOCATION
oceans around the world

FIRST DESCRIBED BY
Johann Philipp Breyne

GLOSSARY

apex predators—animals at the top of the food chain that are not preyed upon by other animals

beaks—the mouths of orthocones

Cambrian period—the first period of the Paleozoic era that occurred between 541 million and 485 million years ago

cephalopods—ocean animals that have tentacles and move by pushing water away from their bodies

chambers—small spaces inside things

evolved—changed over a long period of time

extinct—no longer living

fossils—remains of living things that lived long ago

Paleozoic era—a time in history that happened about 541 million to 252 million years ago; many new kinds of ocean life appeared during the Paleozoic era.

prey—animals that are hunted by other animals for food

tentacles—long, bendable arms of an animal that are used for grabbing things or moving

To Learn More

At the Library

Moening, Kate. *Sea Scorpions.* Minneapolis, Minn.: Bellwether Media, 2023.

Rice, Dona Herweck. *Color-Changing Cephalopods.* Huntington Beach, Calif.: Teacher Created Materials, 2019.

Taylor, Charlotte. *Digging Up Sea Creature Fossils.* New York, N.Y.: Enslow Publishing, 2022.

On the Web

Factsurfer.com gives you a safe, fun way to find more information.

1. Go to www.factsurfer.com.

2. Enter "orthocones" into the search box and click 🔍.

3. Select your book cover to see a list of related content.

INDEX

apex predators, 12
beaks, 7, 10, 11
bodies, 7
cephalopods, 5, 15, 19
chambers, 8
Earth, 17
eggs, 14
evolved, 17
extinct, 17
eyes, 7
food, 10, 11
fossils, 18, 19
get to know, 20–21
Late Cambrian period, 5
map, 5, 19
mosasaurs, 12
oceans, 17
Paleozoic era, 5
prey, 10, 11, 15
pronunciation, 4
scientists, 18, 19
sharks, 12
shells, 5, 6, 7, 8, 13, 14, 15
size, 6, 7, 12
tentacles, 7, 10
United States, 19
young, 14, 15

The images in this book are reproduced through the courtesy of: Mat Edwards, front cover, pp. 1, 2-3, 4-5, 6-7, 8-9, 10-11, 12-13, 14-15, 16-17, 18-19, 20-21; Deidre Woollard/ Wikipedia, p. 19 (fossil); Johann Philipp Breyne/ Wikipedia, p. 21 (fossil drawing).